Aching sunsets

and shimmering dawns

Aching sunsets
and shimmering dawns

SHRUTI GOSWAMI

Hawakal
PUBLISHERS

New Delhi | Calcutta

Hawakal Publishers

70-B/9 Amritpuri, East of Kailash, New Delhi 65
33/1/2 K B Sarani, Mall Road, Calcutta 80

Email info@hawakal.com
Website www.hawakal.com

Cover art by Shutterstock

Cover designed by Bitan Chakraborty

First edition: February 2021

Copyright 2021 © Shruti Goswami

ISBN: 978-81-950350-1-4

Price: INR 350 | USD 10.99

for
Diego Armando Maradona,
El Pibe de Oro

For the joy you brought with your magic feet and
defined my childhood and growing years.
May your legacy live on.

CONTENTS

Endless — 9
A Bare Soul — 10
Recurring Souls — 11
Life and Death — 12
Good Old Human — 13
Masked — 14
Joke — 16
It could have been I — 17
Morbid — 19
Playing Dead — 21
Crowded — 22
Words Within — 24
Reflection — 26
Sparkling Dark — 27
Waiting — 28
Static — 29
Abandoned — 30
Redundant — 32
Innately Alive — 33
Pardon — 34
Timeless — 35
Calling Blues — 36
Devoured — 37
Torrent — 39
All that I ever Want — 40
She Became Love — 41
Leftover Hopes — 42
Guardian Angels — 44
Desires — 45
Calendar of Life — 46
Faded — 47
Heaven Underneath — 48
Bleeding Wine — 49
A Lifetime — 50

Me and Mine   51
By All Means, Don't Bleed   53
Storms   54
Seeped Inside   55
Illicit   56
Uninhibited   57
Dashes and Dots   58
I Rise   59
Thirst   60
Dark   61
What's Left of Me   62
Abandoned   63
Not a Woman Anymore   64
Tangled   66
Midnight   67
Trickledown   68
Retort   69
Slut   70
Consent   71
Blessing   72
Eternity   73
Living like Dead   75
Perished Words   76
Tunnel of Thoughts   77
Valentine   78
Adorn Me   79
Dream's Acre   80
Naked Soul   81
Mirror   82
Chimera   84
Gruesome Goodbye   85
Empty Minds   86
Love or Die   87
Turmoil   89
Alone and Within   90
Mrs. Smith   91

ENDLESS

Some nights are long
Long enough to burn aching hearts
Where raging fires fail,
The fire that warms my hearth
Is the same one that scorch even rains,
As long as the sun rises
The moon beams
And the waves glitter at night,
Some nights seemingly endless
Will always behold dawn at sight.

A BARE SOUL

You are drowning
Neck deep in debt
Favours and money,
Nothing can keep you afloat
The soul that yearns for a touch
Can't be bought;
The deep dark soil awaits
You have to come empty handed
To embrace your love
Or death, whichever you sought
Yet, the writing on the wall is clear:
You need to lose to gain all that you found
A bare soul, awash in the rains.

RECURRING SOULS

Some nights float by
Like fading clouds
With dreams of a castle
And a glass of wine,
The glory of battles won
Preceded by rivers of blood
For those who do not live
To see another sunrise.

Let me embrace your soul
And ease the pain
Tomorrow is another day
For a new sunrise to come again.

LIFE AND DEATH

Death lies, waiting
Beneath dark soils;
Life springs a green
Swan song of paradise.

GOOD OLD HUMAN

Nothing surprises me anymore,
It's like I have given up war,
For a long awaited peace,
For the futility of making people do,
What they never want to
Of making people say, what they never intend,
And all the promises, that were either not made,
Or made and broken
It's like a token
Of something that will never bear fruit
Conflicts and resolutions now decided by brawn,
Dehumanized assertions based on gains to cajol
Trading all the values imbibed,
Is it all for nothing?
Yes, nothing,
Nothing,
Makes me yearn, or wait, the learn complete
The only thing that can surprise now
Is a good old human
The kind I knew when I was young.

MASKED

I wear a veiled smile,
So does the world,
My masked emotions are betrayed
Only through my eyes,
So when you asked on a rainy day
When the showers were as dense as the clouds
And I, alone, longing and yearning for a human touch
I could only reply, "I am fine,"
I hoped my voice did not betray over the phone
For I know my eyes would, if you were home.
You believed me, and for once I wished,
You didn't, and could come snuggle up with a book
With me, on the settee
Beside the window,
Watching the smokes rise from the showers
Through the smoke of hot steaming tea.
Only sighs escape, as the distance that's overbearing
For an unknown devil, invisible,
Threaten and loom over such little conversations,
Longings and yearnings

That virtual touch could never replace.
I wish I could escape with you
Into a mask-less space
With a mask-less face,
In a different world,
That's just ours.

JOKE

I am glad
You took it as a joke
Like every other thing
That made my life worth living
Those feelings, emotions
Verbose and muted
Every damn thing was just a joke
That could be scorned, ridiculed and trampled on
Like a cornered dog, those jokes could get serious
Serious enough to seek, kill for
Or die.
Before you smile, contemplate
Maybe the joke was all mine.

IT COULD HAVE BEEN I

Two little girls
Played outside
I watched with a dull languor
A coffee cup in my hand,
Suddenly, out of nowhere a woman appeared
Chided the white skinned and dragged her aside;
To me, they looked a perfect set of yin and yang,
For the woman, it was a different song that rang
Through her mind,
And I,
I couldn't breathe inside.

It was a cut throat moment
When both the man and the woman
Fit the bill for the job,
Leaders, orators and technical know how
The woman, a tad more experienced, perhaps,
The compensation she asked seemed a bit too much
So she was refused.
While I sat at the desk, the board offered the same

To the man, that the woman was denied,
He was aboard,
And I,
I couldn't breathe inside.

The little boy stuttered,
His mother tongue was different
From the children around him,
His English broken,
The little ones made fun of him
Refused to play
He was the joker of the day
Each and every day, he tried
There was no way he could mingle,
Cold and withdrawn
Forsaken and forlorn
It was too late when his little body was found
Lying on the ground, huddled by the side
And I,
I couldn't breathe inside.

I couldn't die,
Even when, in front of my eyes,
A little bit of humanity wasted away
I was no better than the rest, I can't lie
Complicit, in the injustices that I can't deny
Waiting for someone to take charge
When that someone,
That someone could have been I.

MORBID

Once I hit rock bottom
I realized, dead men don't dream
And those around them
Are as dead as a dried branch of tree
Waiting to be broken off and dispersed
In the wind;
A lot of deaths occurred over a period of time:
Death of love, trust, not being human
Was morbid enough
But then one can't choose the hand dealt out
By fate, God, whatever you may say
So when I looked up from the bottom of the pit
Numbed by the sunlight that hit
My eyes,
I saw these dead bodies floating around me.
The people who killed them were standing at the top
Screaming their lungs out so that I could hear
We want you to live! Have a good life!
But that's not for us to give,
We can just take away those very things

That you learnt assiduously
Come now, let up your hand and let us help you
Start a new life, even though you cannot trust us,
Love us; believe in us, neither can we;
Even with my broken pieces, I was no more whole
I shuddered to think what might be,
If I gave in to their lies.
I closed my eyes, and preferred to die once again
Silently inside.

PLAYING DEAD

Sometimes, I like to play dead.
Like, when the birds forget to sing
And they put egg yolk on avocados
Like the blank stares of walls or
The gathering of dust on a book not opened;
But I am reminded;
Of the cat I forgot to cuddle because I was in a rush
The baby in a pram who was too cute to be resisted,
The groceries waiting to be picked up
On my way back home,
And the home, waiting for me,
With a brilliant orange hue like aspersions cast away
And within that home, the people waiting for me
To have a sip of hot coffee
Or share an anecdote, desperately
Where do they fit in, when I play dead?

CROWDED

The way we have denied each other
Seems way too perfect
It would put strangers to shame
What provocation could not achieve
Distance could,
The body and the mind
Reside and repel like
Two people staying under the same roof
Growing weary of each other;
There's some silence sprinkled all over
Generously like salt,
Makes the wounds stare back, afresh.

Maybe we wanted it that way.
Our lives are too crowded
There are a lot of people
Living between you and me
You let them in.

You are fond of crowds, I detest

The more I do, the more crowded it gets.
The more you do, I retreat,
It started a long time back;
I am, still retreating, probably shall
For the rest of my life;
But when you finally decide to extend a hand
For being by my side, or pulling me to yours
I shall be in another world, another space and time.
You shall be released,
Something you wanted the most
Amidst crowds, wandering, yet never lost.

WORDS WITHIN

I don't know which a greater sin is
The storms hiding darkness, or words hidden within
I know,
The clouds I smoked in a cigar,
Could have created havoc,
Yet I let them drift away
Let them be;
The smokes could never have given
Birth to whirlwinds anyway,
Like words can, even when they drift away
I see
How it hurts until it hurts no more,
Words, storms all pass away
Somewhere, I just feel glad that even today
You remember, I love the taste of
Blackberries in my mouth,
When others have let my love pass by so easily
Like I let the storm pass away.

I am done.

Done being the first to call,
The first to message
The first to remember
The first to fall in
And out of love.

I am done, waiting and wanting
Dreaming and panting
Of things that could never be
Done, wishing till death, warmth of your flesh
Done with empty beds, that stares at me.

I am done, loving like no other
Lusting like there's no other
Done begging and pining
Done, doing all the things, to the moon and back
Done, being the morning sun.

At the end, I am done,
Thinking this was a one of a kind love,
Done hoping, done looking,
Just some sprinkled stars,
In the sky above.

REFLECTION

Autumn's broke this season
Maple leaves beneath abandoned seats,
Seeking shelter when the trees refused to keep 'em,
Swept away by the wind, only remembered when
Tears drop
In silence from above,
Giving them hope, and a reason;
For when the sun sets, the blood orange of the
Horizon seeps into the moon
And stains it like the maple leaves,
Those abandoned, see their reflection,
In the magic of still waters,
The moon meticulously weaves.

SPARKLING DARK

There is darkness in the lights
And darkness is a shade of your nude lips
Creating light
When they rub accidentally.
There's always a spark.

WAITING

Threadbare,
Like the golden moon reflecting on the waters
Of a pristine beach
Without remorse or pride,
The bitter sweet tunes of Shehnai
Wafting in the air, somewhere two bodies
Merge as one,
Melancholy now has a new name
In between, I weave you with my loneliness
Like the moonlight and the waves
They have each other, while I wait
For wait, for me, is a lifelong game.

STATIC

I sit, with just myself,
Ignoring the entire material world,
The morning alarm, the daily chores,
Shopping and eating,
Everything lies abandoned,
And I simply sit there, with myself.
I sit and watch as the migratory birds
Form a pattern in the sky and disappear as they fly,
Imagine myself, flying towards an unknown destination,
With no one to call, no coming back for someone,
No feeling down,
Slowly, everything around me turns misty eyed
Tears, rage and touchiness,
So, I abandon everything and sit with just myself,
Looking at the sky, I entrust me to myself,
My well being, anxiety,
Doubts and thoughts are just mine,
Suddenly, I look down and see,
A swarm of red ants, surround a static me.

ABANDONED

The day when they took Hossain for the burial,
I started my preparations too,
Some things, habits and
Memories needed to be buried,
I know not who Hossain was,
So it wasn't a surprise
When my eyes were dry even when
I saw his procession being taken,
But I died a thousand times in my mind,
Simply in the process of preparing endless lists.

I remember, watches were a favourite of mine,
So when you threw them away once,
A zillion moments, memories of love, time
Were lost in darkness.
And then, then I berated myself,
And buried that very longing.
Today, I watch from afar,
Never adorn my hand anymore.

I remember, for days and nights,
I had stared at my phone,
Waiting for just a reply from you,

And had even imagined answers to those replies,
Which never came,
And even those were unanswered,
Only, my words and wait compounded indefinitely,
And still, there was no answer,
I never imagined, somewhere else,
Your replies were rushing every moment,
Every waking hour of the day,
Just that, they never came to me, even for once.
When I was almost dead from the mental pain
And agony that peace seemed like
A mirage to my mind,
I decided, no more,
The wait must be buried,
My replies would be only for those
Who despite their busy schedule
Wrote back to me without any reason,
Asked me questions
Without any reason too, and I;
I will reply.

Gradually, as I started to abandon
And bury these habits,
These things one by one
I realized I have nothing left to bury anymore,
There wasn't any work left to do,
So I decided once more to exhume
Their skeletons and burn them to ashes
And immerse them in water,
So that they have no way left to return.

The only good thing is,
They would rather they did not return as well.

REDUNDANT

At the end
Between the embraces of arms
And the heavy damp breaths
Everything seeks closure;
Hopes rise and fall amidst heaving breasts
Only hoping that the unseen tears
That falls in the dark,
Our deepest secrets and our greatest fears
Melt away together, just like our bare bodies melt
Trying to reach out to each other.
Words were rendered redundant.

INNATELY ALIVE

Sometimes, at night
I feel like a firefly
When there's no light,
I burn like hell inside
Yet the innate glow
That keeps on flashing
Intermittently
Reminds me, till I die
The burn only keeps me wanting
Keeps me alive.

PARDON

Tomorrow's the end
And we have asked for your blessings, love,
Above all, forgiveness for our sins
From tomorrow, we shall be back
To our routine, the city and its djinns
Shall watch us with unequivocal horror
How we transition from being a worshipper of power
To a harasser, abuser and molester, every hour
But then, didn't we already beg your pardon?
That's all you can expect, that's all there is, to begin.

Footnote: written during Bengali's biggest festival, the *Durga Puja* where the female deity is worshipped for 5 days as a goddess but abused and molested for the rest of the year, a recurring irony.

TIMELESS

I go far
Farther away
I draw close
Close to you
In a way
As life swings
The seasons it brings
Draws me back
To this earth and beyond
What lies,
I give you what no woman could give
Like love, time defies
Flowers blossom in
Timeless springs.

CALLING BLUES

There's no one to call and ask
Why didn't you call, anymore;
Just endless nights in neat little boxes
Counting on pains and sorrows to keep company
Sometimes, desperately hanging on to them
To fill up the void
Of voiceless nameless faces that once called up,
Even by mistake;

It was one such evening when the door was closed
And shut forever
One by one, the voices died down
Now they all drown
In artificial fountains that smell like roses and jasmines,
While a lone finger hang on,
Hovering over the button to receive a call
That will never come.

DEVOURED

I feed on you.
Your thoughts, your dreams, your smile and
Tears
I feed on them all.
Until you start thinking
Behaving like I was a blood sucking parasite.

Forgetting, once you begged for this
Now, you bask in denial
Forgetting that you too
Feed on me.

It's symbiotic,
But not to your heart's content.

You devoured me,
While I feasted.
Let's give each other back
Everything we have of the other.
Somewhere in the process,

We became a little like each other.

Probably a lot.

A lot which can never be unfed.

TORRENT

I have stopped counting my sorrows,
They are always hazy
Like misty eyes,
I have stopped counting my blessings too
I do not know where they reside.

Floods come, and they go
The deluge can't be stopped
The bridges I burnt, the dams I broke
Who stopped by,
I'll never know.

ALL THAT I EVER WANT

It's not what's on my mind,
It's the thousands of other things
That aren't,
In a bid to embrace what's not mine
I forget what I want.
Forever is not the end, never
All that I ever want,
Is what I want it for.

SHE BECAME LOVE

She became love,
Even before love came
She was love, and love
Was not a name
For in love, like love's own
She loved like love
Could never be shown
She was love, and love found her
In love that could never be shown.
She became love
Love was her,
Her very own.

LEFTOVER HOPES

Before I left, I forgot to arrange the bed sheets,
The bed remains unmade, there was no time left,
The bedcover too has some creases, here and there,
I know you wouldn't mind,
But it's an old habit, and habits die hard,
That's not to say I have kept leftovers in the fridge,
I haven't, just the way you like,
The creases that do appear inside the mind,
Don't smell stale
Clean like a slate,
The dried rose petals that once waited in an old book
Was also set free today.
It's stale as hell for you as well,
When youth fades,
There's little to be done with that what's left,
Oh, I forgot to say,
The keys to the almirah remain at the same place
From where you once lovingly put in my hands,
Just took some old pictures,
Of which you have little use,

But for me, I take memories.

Your home shall wait for you,
But so will some leftover hopes,
Sorrows and a heart full of woes.

GUARDIAN ANGELS

Life is like a piece of moon,
Waxing and waning,
It starts with the full moon
Slowly, devoured by darkness.
The new moon looks like
A misfit among the sparkling stars,
Is someone home? Who goes past by?
The pitch black darkness which seems never ending
Yet the waves of the sea come rushing by,
Hungry to lap up every bit of the moon
Beams that disappear,
But the onus is on both,
One loses his way, another drowns in despair
Only, like guardian angels,
The stars sparkle in the sky.

DESIRES

Some rains drown the tears that well up
Others set your heart on fire;
Whether you will lament
Or claim the moment,
Is not just a decision
It's the deepest secret,
The innermost desire.

CALENDAR OF LIFE

Never looked back to see
All the black and yellow and blue days
Some circled, marked, some crossed
Pages turned, behold! A whole month gone;
Just the bold reds stand out
Showing a red flag to the bull
But she doesn't come charging, those remain
As mere memories of bygones
She once celebrated
The reds mean nothing anymore.

Except perhaps, some dried blood from
Wounds still sore.
Each day passes by, the calendar says
Do not return, yet she does
Every single day
Of her paused life.

FADED

Everyone I know is leaving.
Everyone, one by one, leaves eventually.
Leaving foot prints, broken hearts, mossy
Emotions, pretty dandelions
Leaving a sigh, untold goodbye, dried eyes
Leave emotions, in a dark night sky.
I know of people who never left, even though
They intended to,
Of people who simply stayed because they
Had nowhere to go
Uncertainty is the biggest gallows, one fears to
Walk into until one is pushed, pushed hard
Then there are some who pretended to stay,
They left even before they could come in,
Invited or not is a different question
They never left a thing, except darkness,
That eventually swallowed them up like a
Black hole, even time was lost on them.

Everyone I know of, are leaving.
Leaving to, from, something.

HEAVEN UNDERNEATH

The roads that lead to heaven are not
Sprinkled with gold
It's a rain kissed path, with no bridges
No footpaths with tiled ground
Await the touch of feet
And the heaven, that's not above in the sky
Neither in the depths of oceans or under
Shady twilight,
It's the throbbing heart, underneath.

BLEEDING WINE

And suddenly I find a box
Containing a set of wine openers
The box, unopened
For the wine bottles that we dreamt of toasting with
For every step we take,
The bottles, unopened, not bought
For you, I was just an afterthought that
Needed nothing to be toasted to,
It was just addiction all the way,
When you said I love you
Love you did, but t'was the drink that spoke thus,
In reality, the emotions were simply bottled up,
Like the wines,
And you drank all the way to your freedom
Like nothing else mattered.
I still wait with the unopened bottles
Shall wait till the emotions die,
Hoping that a day will arrive
When the numbers won't matter a bit
Just, the wine inside.

A LIFETIME

The rains had something to tell
The evening, lit by yellow lamps, quivering,
Flickering flames, as we held hands
The exhaustion of sojourn was
Calmed by a balmy wind
The rains caressed our hearts,
How long has it been since we had such an eve?
Where gloominess faded
With the sound of rain and the smell of mud?
Probably another lifetime.
I lived a lifetime today.

ME AND MINE

There was a time;
I looked away from occurrences
As though they were mere deviations,
Those times grew up faster than I could,
Like black magic, they became more frequent and gory
I still hated those times,
They made me feel like
A prisoner of my own tame mind
I wouldn't have given a single dime
To make them feel real, magic to me,
Was always sublime,
And as they happened,
I looked up to have a peak
At the stationed bosses in the sky
I still thought it's not me, not mine,
But my pigeon returned
With the message and it was then,
Then that I felt, turning blind while still breathing,
Still alive is a crime
Now I see them happen, real time
I see you, hiding behind curtains

Of uncertainty in your own character,
A backbone bent back in time,
Let's come back home,
Only together this time.

BY ALL MEANS, DON'T BLEED

You should look married
But you must not bleed
We have a problem with your bleeding you see,
If you didn't bleed,
We wouldn't be harboring murderers and thieves
But you must look married for we like to feel
She's owned by someone,
Hence there's nothing to conquer and own
Unless you look married,
We fail to realize that you are off limits, off the market
For whoever heard of consent of an unmarried one?
You must look married,
Whether you choose or not, it doesn't matter as well
But we can pretend you chose to,
For our well being and longevity
For those who don't, don't care about their spouses,
But we have no such obligation to be,
Even the State agrees to it, and you call it regressive,
When looking married comes free for you,
Bleeding is still a sin
Look married, by all means, just do not bleed.

(written when there was GST imposed on sanitary napkins
but not sindoor)

STORMS

Storms are mighty dangerous, and lovely
Like a necessary evil, bringing in respite
But the collateral damage
Is far more than one could bargain for
Yet, secretly wishing for more.
For the allure of a steaming hot cup
On a rainy day with the storm beating at the sills
Surpasses images of sheets, tattered and torn,
And the hapless figures drenched, forlorn
Digging into romance like a dagger drawn.
Storms are carefully bred, not born.

SEEPED INSIDE

Sometimes, sandstorms hide more than they reveal,
The blemishes cleverly concealed
Only some drops of rain,
As incisive as a barb can drill through
Turning the desert into an oasis.
It's a raw deal,
For many a traveller in his quest to rule the world
Fell prey to his own thirst.

Poison, they say runs deep,
And the scars bled underneath
The oasis a mere pool of bloodied water
A desert rose sprouting beneath
As sandstorms hid all that was there to hide
Another drop, just another one,
Seeped inside.

ILLICIT

I embraced you, after a long time
In my dreams
All this while, I had been sitting beside you,
Glancing at the rear view mirror, for a hint,
A surge of feelings swept my mind
I felt numb.
Should I have? Did you too?
You must have,
For how else could I throw
Caution to the winds and hold you so tight
You could hardly breathe
I gazed into your eyes, longingly, in two minds,
And then
Decided to shy away from that one kiss,
That would have sealed our connection
For the world to call it illicit.

UNINHIBITED

For the uninhibited,
Uninitiated bouts of passion don't die
Don't choke on emotions;
They freely flow like love,
And transform into words,
That's a poem in itself.
Because love doesn't die.
Lovers do.
Or maybe, they don't, too.

DASHES AND DOTS

Come ASAP. Stop. I am dying. Stop.
Thus ran the last dashes and dots,
Not knowing,
Who the recipient of the ill fated note was,
Whose life's gonna end at a full stop,
Not knowing, alas,
Even its death was as imminent,
As the last telegram of the country was sent.

(When the last telegraph office of this country was shut down)

I RISE

I wore an invisible cape
Every time I was broken and I felt I could not rise,
Almost drowning, and then,
Just like magic, it was me
Me, who held together the pieces,
Broken from inside
I rise,
Those tears,
That mourned the loss of a child that could be,
Or a fatherless child abandoned at birth
I wept,
I did not pray, there's no one I know for certain,
Who could heal,
Only myself, I could seek,
Consolations are mere words;
I wanted all of them to feel my heart,
Broken, just like theirs,
I believe, we all are made
From the same flesh and blood
And they simply shape up differently, like we need
Yet the magic remains, and a sense of belonging,
Your grief is mine, in you I see
A different me, every time.

THIRST

The seas are calling
Thirsty, they haven't had a drop to drink for as
Long as they remember,
From someone who loves them
Finds in them, her home,
I must go, to the home where the sky and the
Seas seal their kiss
And quench their lifelong thirst;
I must go, for there lay my home
And their life,
They need a drop of life, to feel alive
Like some private emotions that can't be seen.
Let me make their life, mine.

DARK

Birds chirp, it's hardly spring
Flowers bloom in fear, showers
Pour in, acid rain.

WHAT'S LEFT OF ME

Probably I put it the wrong way.
Maybe, I should've asked,
Are you so busy that you can't watch
The flowers bloom?
Instead, I retorted, you could never find the
Time to grow old with me, but you shall pay
For it someday or the other.
Maybe, I should've asked, if I really mattered
To you, would you keep waiting
For an opportune moment to come
And meet me?
Instead, I barked, if I was that important,
You wouldn't have kept me waiting.
All this, and much more, of what could've
Been and what had been,
But you see, when over the years,
The patience is tested and tried, relationships
Played with,emotions trampled,
I've died a thousand deaths, and now,
Not me,
What's left of me, speaks.

ABANDONED

The wind left a taste of saltiness on the tongue
Probably trying to remind of a silent love
Latently spread across the length and width of life
Turning a desert life into pools of oasis.
But the wind moves on, the wetness disappears
Abandoned houses and streets are all that remain.

NOT A WOMAN ANYMORE

I have hit a dead end.
I have been hit, hard.
Punched harder.

Neglected like I didn't exist.

Even my birth scorned;
Something that I had no choice in.

Made to look like I was being doled out favours
Made to look like I should be begging
For the air I breathe in
Made to look that the privilege
I have is owned by someone
Who was being just kind to me.

Asked to leave all and come running,
While there would be no leaving anything worth leaving
And feel Thankful that I have been asked to leave
All this, like I bargained for them,

And now I should feel happy that
I am getting a softer deal,
I may have forgiven, but the scars don't heal
Not so rapidly, like the blinking of an eye
Like a missed heartbeat.

No, it's not that sweet.

Forgive me, for my inability to act like
I don't know what I deserve,
To be naive, to the core,
To act like I am not bothered by the
Scars that digs deep and makes me bleed,
It's not like I would follow, and you would lead,
To get some, you give some, and then,
You give some more,
Instead, you hurt me, till I was sore,
Being pretentious,
And oblivious of the lies didn't help that much,
I'd rather I had picked up the swords to fight it all out,
And watch
My bastion re-heal itself,
While you wore an armour made from my love,
My flesh and blood,
I grant you this inequality, I am a born fighter,
I would go into this naked, wearing all blows
On my body like jewels on a queen's bod,
A fighter is born,
I'm not a woman, not anymore.

TANGLED

How do you calculate the mess you're in?
Tangled knot of threads, thrown away
That's how it is with the mess
It's never untied
You hide it inside
And wait, for someone to find it
Embrace it and untangle it gently
Just to show that a mess can be loved too.

One just needs someone to show
You are not really a mess
Just fighting with your inner demons and angels
Who refuse to let go.

MIDNIGHT

Midnight ascends like a sorcerer
The moon stealthily passes by
Like it's afraid, very afraid
But would surely deny;

Some stars fall off
They have a long way to go
Light trapped, zapped in matter
Like some fragile, bruised ego.

The stars and the moon dance and preen
On the walls of a home
That they now call their own.

TRICKLEDOWN

9 a.m. The coffee is late.
I curse it because it took so much of my precious time.
Wine would have been much better, I rued.
The car honked impatiently.
Am I the only one who needs
To be reminded that I am late, that I need to run?
Yet, why should I, to whom, I say.
It's just a trickledown effect. I console myself.
The coffee's late. Hence I am.
Doesn't the sun rise late too, in the winters?
Does it dawn at the exact time, everyday?
I wait like a project in a pipeline, waiting to happen,
If I may
The road runners can steal the show, for now,
As I patiently wait for that day.

RETORT

The waves that once caressed your feet
Now hits you back angrily,
For the sea returns back
What you gave it, manifold
Just like a woman who had enough of it.

SLUT

Damaged.

Some damages are permanent.
Like the ones which were made when you
Called her a slut,
A whore
Maybe something more.

You cannot drain an ocean of patience
Or break the highest peak,
You can drown or swim
You can climb and win
The damages stay with her, the woman you
Abused,
Each day, worse and worse.

When the worst comes
And she leaves, you might well discover
The damage was all yours.

CONSENT

The power, they say, lie in a lot of things,
Money, truth, beauty and what not,
Try it lady, just a "No" would suffice
To know consent cannot be bought.

(Written after the #metoo movement)

BLESSING

Blades of grass graze against each other
Unmindful of the storm that would raze them,
A raindrop here a raindrop there,
A blessing has been granted.

ETERNITY

I shall be floating in snowflakes
In case you are wondering where
You'll catch me when I fall,
It's gonna be a silent night, with just some snow,
That's all,
And in between every waking hour,
And every moment when I sleep
You can find some snowflakes for me,
Just for keeps,
I shall keep them warm,
In between cold sheets and blankets,
Till you come to reclaim them for posterity
Or maybe, love me when I am numb,
For every night ends with a new sun,
Every day with a new moon,
Every moment that I spend pining for you,
It feels right
Just like eternity.

How many bombs would finally settle
The score about the fact that we are

Inhumans and have rendered ourselves unfit
To be even breathing in this civilized (?) world
That the little bodies that fit within two arms
Are our own children, who slept too early
Never to wake up,
That those who perpetrate it still have red
Wine or a cognac for dinner and a good
Morning on their lips for their own families
Before they order another round of bombing
As good morning messages
No matter how far you rise, you rinse and
Bathe with the blood of countless ones
Because you are not humans,

Just vultures in disguise.

LIVING LIKE DEAD

I am afraid of deaths.
Now that's not a normal thing.
Coz I am afraid of people dying around me
And I see, I am the last one to go
And there's no one to share my sunsets with
No one to say, I told you so
It's lonely out there, when you are left behind alone
Reminiscing memories, trying to create some more.
I am afraid of deaths.
That's not normal.

Just like someone living.

PERISHED WORDS

Have all the poems died?
To wait for someone to reside
In the depths of heart require unfathomable
Patience in disguise
But the one who does not wait, is waited for by none,
And so goes the word around
Heaven and peace are just a state of mind
There's nothing divine;
For some words have died, and those left,
Left to wonder,
Whether it was worth their time.

Death should never come as a surprise.

TUNNEL OF THOUGHTS

The tunnel had ended
There was no light at the other end
The door ajar;
Like the room waiting
For someone's footsteps
And touch to close it
It was morning again, somewhere far
At the other end of the world
Hardly something to look forward to
The nights stained with coffee
The cars on their usual midnight escapades
Panting, exhausted in delight
Passengers look on with indifference,
The cents reeked of something intoxicating
As fingers embraced each other, closed down
Pushing 'em far far down the path.

The tunnel opens up.
In another world.

VALENTINE

It's cold. And dark.

Darkness all around.
Just the warmth of your love
And I could die a million times over
Just, this once,
I do not want to die
Before I hear you say
You're mine.

I wanted you
To be my life divine
You, my love
My Valentine.

ADORN ME

I forget the last time I reached out to you
Now, only sighs, untold goodbyes
Rule the roost
The coffee gets cold
Every time I hold it to my lips
And get lost in a reverie,
The world rushes by;

I still wait for the time
When you shall come and hold my hand
Say nothing but feelings
That was tears in disguise,
That adorned a brilliant night like a thousand stars
And a moon:

A moon that outshone the sun.

DREAM'S ACRE

So I prepare the field
Like mass graves
Walk over, inspect
Analyze in retrospect
All those who need to be laid
Carefully, so that even the worms
And the rotting leaves
Do not have an inkling of what lies beneath.

My dreams.

NAKED SOUL

While the city lights dim in the fog of the night
I tried to peel off winter for a cover on my naked soul
And then I remembered,
Homelessness was the trade off
For the path I treaded
Winter was just another skin to peel.

MIRROR

Are you that starved?
Lapping up gory details of violation
Of a little flower
Act by act, scene by scene
Moments and seconds
The shrieks and screams?
Do you want to relive those
That you wanted to
In your mind,
To perpetrate
Yet could not,
Are you trying to find
Whether the victim had enough to wear
A cleavage here and there
Legs perhaps, or sleeveless arms?
Do you still need to relive
(If I told you)
It's a child, her age is under
Five?
Imagine then, what you may

The details day by day
Would you still dig deep
You're sure you wouldn't weep
If the child was yours
To say?

(On the increasing crime on children.)

CHIMERA

I arrange the stars on the night sky
Distant dreams, that deny
A whole night's sleep
Starry nights have fire within
Waiting to burst into flames
And a new beginning;
I come back, arrange my pots and pans
Turn on the flame.

I cook another dream.

GRUESOME GOODBYE

Sometimes, I feel happy about death
Gruesome revenge, served on a platter that's
Beyond human imagination,
I see my face
On every dead woman,
They cry just like I do
And try to reach out, but I am afraid,
Very afraid, I can't bear the touch of
Another human anymore,
At least, in this life,
I would rather be cold, alone, lonely,
Than be touched.

After all, I am a corpse you don't want to touch,
Let's pretend,
I am dead.

Then say goodbye.

EMPTY MINDS

It's been a while
Footsteps that were washed away,
Returned like a haunted soul
I had a feeling I could go on talking like never before
Things that I never said, you never heard
I assumed you did, the wound turned sore
Shadows that I tried to leave behind dragged me
The wall that I tore down, the bridges that I broke
Stood lurking behind closed corridors.

Footsteps follow me around,
I wish you were here, just this time
To rescue me from empty minds and noiseless sounds.
Just once, that would suffice
For a lifetime.

LOVE OR DIE

I never knew I still had some tears that
Could come out when I least expected,
They were tears, no doubt, not blood;
Not plain water one could drink from a cup,
Maybe a woman is an ocean
Where the salty water never dries up
And so I questioned, I didn't know who
What do you call it when you don't believe in love?
Yet want him back,
Huddled close to you without a single word;
When you know that everything,
From the sex you had to the fights fought hard
Was simply chemically programmed
Yet you didn't fit in the evolution theory
And got your heart torn into shreds
And then again, and again
Unless you did not have one,
Or the one you had turned into a stone
Which was offered like a defective
Gene desperate to annihilate itself

And it broke;
Your narcissism was not enough
To boost your self-worth, or what was left of it,
Surprised, that you still want more of him
As if this self destruction wasn't enough to ruin,
But this time, only to cry and cry,
Those tears that weren't there,
For a person who wasn't there,
Yet what would you call it
When you want him so bad,
You could probably drown in
An ocean simply to prove you were ready to die
Or to live another life,
Instead of love?

TURMOIL

There's an uneasy feeling
Rising in my stomach
I wish I could throw up
Pretending it was a baby
But it stuck like a curse
The uneasiness,
Something that gradually makes you feel tired,
Tired of discomfort,
The ears buzzing like an alarm
It's cold outside, and on the inside, warm
Even a yawn gives me goose bumps
And I, I still cannot
Fathom, within the ocean
Whose waves are rising and falling
But never crashing on the beach
Maybe a whirlpool sucking everything in
Might do the trick.

ALONE AND WITHIN

I have been searching for someone
To confess, how much I love him
The corner cafes, the forlorn benches,
Wear a desolate look,
Like they have waited for you to arrive,
Only to be disappointed,
I held on to my fort,
But the words I could barely contain
Gushing forth like a thirsty fountain,
No dearth of water but dying to drink,
Some parts of me give company
To the empty chairs and tables,
Even have a coffee to show off,
Perhaps, it's never too late to begin,
Loving, alone, and within.

MRS. SMITH

My father made a rain house for me
At the other end of the garden.
It took a long long time to build
But he made time
When he was sober,
And not beating his wife.

Whenever a storm brewed, I ran to the rain house,
And watched the rains fall over the glass panes
And doors, and glass openings on the roof
For hours and hours,
I returned only when the sky was clear
And my mom rested in her bed, for days
I never left if the rains started falling
For I was afraid I would get wet;
And I was usually blinded by the tears
And the blood that fell,
Rains, they make me numb as hell.

One day, when the sun shone like it was finally all right

My mom left, my dad was broken
He drank even more
My rain house seldom saw me again;
It was my turn to grow sore
I had grown up
And rain houses were for children,
So I bore
They call my dad as their own dad
And I am Mrs. Smith to them.